P I A N O   S O L O

GAME OF THRONES: ORIGINAL MUSIC FROM THE HBO® SERIES – SEASON 8

MUSIC BY RAMIN DJAWADI

ISBN 978-1-5400-6179-9

For all works contained herein:
Unauthorized copying, arranging, adapting, recording, Internet posting, public performance,
or other distribution of the music in this publication is an infringement of copyright.
Infringers are liable under the law.

Visit Hal Leonard Online at
www.halleonard.com

Contact us:
Hal Leonard
7777 West Bluemound Road
Milwaukee, WI 53213
Email: info@halleonard.com

In Europe, contact:
Hal Leonard Europe Limited
42 Wigmore Street
Marylebone, London, W1U 2RN
Email: info@halleonardeurope.com

In Australia, contact:
Hal Leonard Australia Pty. Ltd.
4 Lentara Court
Cheltenham, Victoria, 3192 Australia
Email: info@halleonard.com.au

GAME OF THRONES

Music by RAMIN DJAWADI

Moderately fast

THE RAINS OF CASTAMERE

Words and Music by RAMIN DJAWADI
and GEORGE R.R. MARTIN

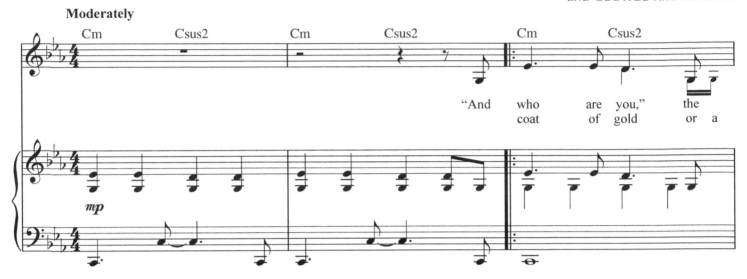

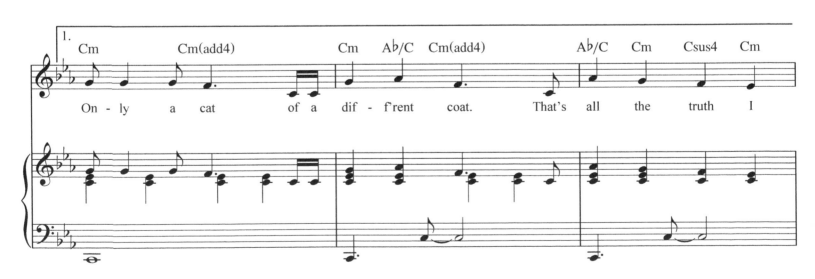

FLIGHT OF DRAGONS

By RAMIN DJAWADI

ARRIVAL AT WINTERFELL

By RAMIN DJAWADI

JENNY OF OLDSTONES

By RAMIN DJAWADI, DAN WEISS,
DAVID BENIOFF and GEORGE RR. MARTION

Moderately slow

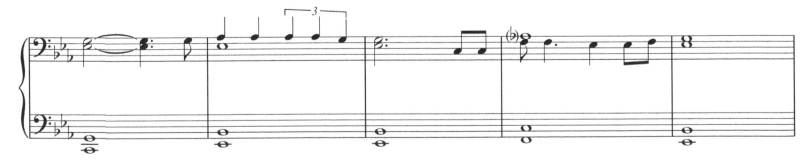

THE NIGHT KING

By RAMIN DJAWADI

THE LAST WAR

By RAMIN DJAWADI

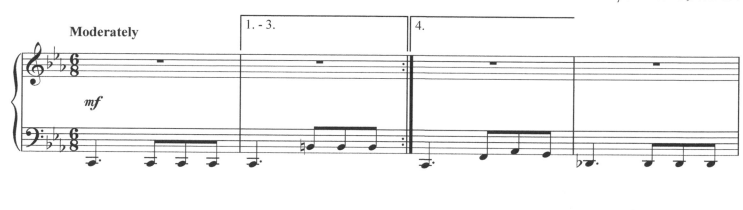

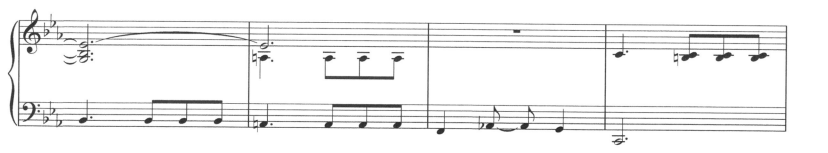

*Use palm of hand to play cluster.

Very slowly, freely

pp

Slowly, expressively

34

Moderately slow, freely

NOT TODAY

By RAMIN DJAWADI

Moderately slow

pp

Pedal ad lib. throughout

STAY A THOUSAND YEARS

By RAMIN DJAWADI

Slowly, expressively

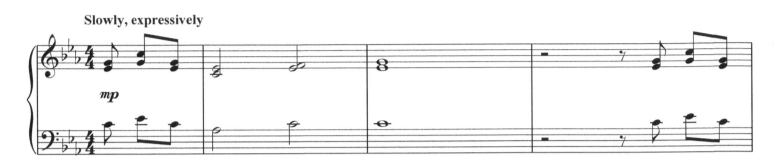

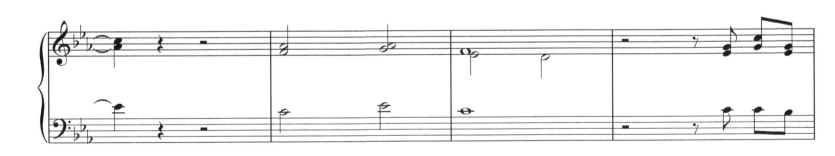

THE IRON THRONE

By RAMIN DJAWADI

Slowly, freely

pp

Pedal ad lib. throughout

Moderately, steadily

THE LAST OF THE STARKS

By RAMIN DJAWADI

Moderately fast